IS AMERICA ON THE BRINK OF SOCIALISTIC COLLAPSE?

IS AMERICA ON THE BRINK OF SOCIALISTIC COLLAPSE?

|||||||||||||||||||||||||||||||||||||||||||||||||||||||||||||||||||||||||||||||||||||||||||||||||||||||||||||||||

ATOS

To order additional copies of this book, contact:
Xlibris LLC
1-888-795-4274
www.Xlibris.com
Orders@Xlibris.com
635813

This book is intended to alert all real Americans that the United States of America is rapidly approaching a point of no return on the inane policies currently employed. And unless we, the people, stop the Washington, DC, crowd from business as usual, we will collapse as a Constitutional Republic in this author's opinion.

PART 1

After a while, even the blind must see how wrong the Democrats are in the direction they are taking this country.

In less than ten days, there have been two articles from Britain on screwed-up surgeries in their Obamacare-type medical program:

1) A woma n went in for an appendectomy. She was pregnant and the doctor removed her ovaries killing both her and her unborn child. Now I'm not a doctor but recalling my Biology from High School, those two organs aren't even close.

2) A man went in for a urinary surgery, and they accidentally gave him a vasectomy,

Oops. Yes, my fellow Americans, this is where we are headed if we don't stop this utter nonsense now.

The author had paid in to Medicare benefits at the maximum rate for thirty-eight years. Now I am being told the Obama Medicare Rationing Board will decide what treatments I can have and not have. This rationing board will be comprised of fifteen non-elected cronies of Barry (whatever his name is, was, or will be). Where the hell is the fairness in that! This program based on the last report from the Federal Government was that this Ponzi scheme, as are all Federal programs, are not getting the younger membership they had hoped for but were getting a big play in enrollment from *Human Immunodeficiency Virus* (HIV) sufferers. So this is perfectly clear: I bought an insurance policy that will not guarantee payoff in benefits after I'm old enough for some political crony to say yea or nay on treatment. In the mean time, I being heterosexual and moral, will be punished for paying into a policy that some immoral gays will enjoy the benefits and illegal aliens will benefit, health wise from my thirty-eight years worth of dollars. "Hogwash," I say. This program, to add a little salt to the wound, was voted on by people who will be exempted from that program. Is this author crazy or is the law that was passed insane? In Britain, where s ocialized medicine has been running rampant since 1961, it has a higher death rate for older people than anything else. Hey, seniors, are you listening? These are the wonderful, thoughtful people you put into office. Well, they are not wonderful or thoughtful: they are political animals and everyone that voted in favor of Obamacare should be thrown out of office and if you want a little old, fashioned tar; and feathering might be in order. Not being a lawyer, it would seem that this is tantamount to "Conspiracy to commit murder," and those who proposed it and wrote it and legislated it should be brought to justice.

Even third-world nations respect their elders but apparently not in the United States of America. is this _____ And to make matters worse, the current administration turned down an opportunity to save money on the program by getting a specialized computer program, as I recall, developed by IBM. They are not even interested in nailing the medical violators. This, my fellow Americans, is politics in the United States of America. Almost like Nazi Germany, only there—it were Jews; here, it's everyone over seventy-five. Shame on you, Democrats. Another interesting point is when our Constitution was drafted, the framers specifically set up three branches of government; so there would be a check and balance system on each branch. This clown in office blows through the Constitution like it isn't there. Why won't the Supreme Court of the United States hear cases that impugn his eligibility? Because there is no precedent for it. Well, guess what, ladies and gentlemen of Supreme Court of the United States? Maybe, just maybe, you have to stick your neck out a little for the American people. You took an oath to serve and protect. Just out of curiosity, "does not hearing the case set a very dangerous precedent for future imposters?" There are thousands of cases that had no precedence, but some judge somewhere did his/ her job. Are we listening Supreme Court of the United States?

Final word on this travesty of Justice, it's an old political trick to only use an opponent's name when it can be associated with something terrible like Obamacare. The other side of the coin is to pay tribute to an individual like the "Salk vaccine" thereby paying tribute to Dr. Jonas Salk. Well, this author thinks we should call it what it is "Holocaust American Style."

PART 2

Let's discuss Muslims for a bit.

As previously stated, the author spent time in Libya and Lebanon in the late 1950s courtesy of the US Government; and when in business, I had the occasion to have them as clients.

Lesson 1: You never stop negotiating price. I don't care if you're in Tripoli buying beautiful jewelry or New Jersey doing an engineering project for them.

Lesson 2: They are shrewd businesspeople, who band themselves together for purchases greater than one family can afford for investments.

Lesson 3: Their culture is very different than ours in some respects; their legal system is based on Sharia Law. A very cruel and painful method (something out of the past): everything is negotiated. Familywise, fairly similar, but the woman is like a second-class citizen. Literally, the women have very little (if any) rights, and beating wives is permitted—plus more than one wife is allowed.

Lesson 4: Their people are (like any culture) with some large quirks. People are people; and you have mild, moderate, and extreme in any culture. But they go one step further to ultra-extreme. It is a very volatile culture as it doesn't take much to whip a mild or moderate guy into a near frenzy by an ultra–extreme. Then look out.

Lesson 5: Again, they take their religion very seriously by praying, as I
recall, five times a day; and then there are different interpretations
of the Quran, depending on whether you're mild or all the way at the
other end of the spectrum: fanatical. Those are the ones you really
have to watch out for, especially if you are an infidel. It's estimated
there are only 30 percent fanatical. Now you must understand that the
Muslim nations comprise roughly 23 percent of the world population
at about 1,600,000,000; and this is broken down into two distinct
factions, *Sunni* and *Shiite*, who have been at odds with one another
since Mohammad's death around AD 600. Fortunately, the Sunnis
are the larger group and generally more tempered, but they also have
their extremist; hence, give or take a few million, there are roughly 480
million extremists in the world, and that's where there is a problem
worldwide. There are many different factions within each group that
shift like the wind in Florida on an irregular basis.

It's my opinion that the best way to control is to make a firm stand like
Russia and Australia, i.e. : "This is our country not yours; you will obey our
rules and laws or leave." Simple yet direct. The strange part is they leave
their country for one reason or another; namely, peace and yet try to instill
their rules. Well, logically, that just doesn't make any sense. If you are not
happy where you are and come here, why try to establish your rules that
you left to get away from. Already in several states in this country, they
are establishing Sharia Law. My attitude: "No way. Our country, our rules
and laws or leave." This being Mr. / Mrs. Nice Person does not work in
this world anymore, especially when dealing with different cultures. They
interpret it as a sign of weakness.

All cultures have a sensitive point, mainly in the Far East, Middle East,
and Europe. The W estern nations—it's not as strong as there. Primarily,
family honor is on top of their list, and unclean animals especially in the

Muslim world—they won't even travel with unclean animals. Israel, in order to stop Palestinian terrorist bombings in 2000, started hanging pig lard in buses, malls, and other places that had been previous targets. Hell, back in 1911 when "Black Jack" Pershing was in the Philippines and they were getting Muslim terrorist attacks, he captured a number of them, had them dig their own graves, then had them tied to poles and shot—all but one. Oh, he had his troops kill pigs first, dip their bullets in the blood, and then shot them. Afterward, they buried them in the grave they had dug and spread the mutilated pig remnants over the bodies and then covered the grave. The released Muslim went back and reported exactly what had happened. As martyrs, they couldn't get into heaven because they were unclean because of the tainted bullets and the unclean animal carcasses on their bodies. Result: terrorist attacks stopped.

Now, if we advertised each flight was carrying an unclean animal in the cargo hold, terrorists would not fly, and we could cut the size of the Transportation Security Administration (TSA). So as not to punish all Muslims, we could advertise *no unclean animals in cargo hold* and have Transportation Security Administration do their number only on those flights. Sounds a little gross, but are we trying to save money and combat terrorists tit for tat or not! It would seem to this author that the Muslims might be inconvenienced a little, but better for all the rest of us all the time.

Just think: no more going to the airport two hours earlier! Always go for their weak points.

PART 3

How about a bit on our foreign policy?

As previously mentioned in other editions, our foreign policy seems to be "throw more money at the situation," and we all know that it isn't working nor will it work except for Washington, DC. It's like "Monkey see; Monkey do" administration after administration and always on Mr. & Mrs. John Q. Publics back in taxes. We are probably the most hated country in the world for our interference in their affairs and having so much wealth.

Here's an amusing little story attributed to Slick Willie Clinton. I don't know its validity: Right after 9/11/01 and the drop in airline traffic sales, purportedly Slick Willie suggested all stewardesses go naked because Muslims were not supposed to view other naked women other than his spouse—same principle as I'm suggesting!

It seems Washington, DC, thinks the taxpayers in this country are a bottomless well of money; however, nothing can be further from the truth. It's difficult not to read an article about this or that longtime business going out of business, the latest of which was Barnes and Noble. Why? Not enough disposable income beyond necessities, problem with too much tax, not enough jobs, too much wasted government spending.

If you will take a pause and give me a little leeway here, the author will prove that past and current Government policies were wrong. Being a firm believer in history is the future.

1) Confucius—"give a man a bowl of rice and you will feed him for a day; teach him how to grow his own rice and you save his life."

2) Thessalonians 3:10—"he who does not work neither shall he eat."

3) John Smith-Jamestown (1609)—"You must obey this now for a law that he that will not work shall not eat (except by sickness or he be disabled). For the labors of 30 or 40 honest and industrious men shall not be consumed to maintain 150 idle loiterers."

4) These words of wisdom which have transgressed time both BC & AD are the answer to our problems as both Hunter Hearst Helmsley and John Fitzgerald Kennedy knew when they started the Peace Corp.

5) We should rewrite the purported LBJ's "Put down your shovels, sit on your asses, light up a Camel as this is the promised land" to something like "Put out your Camel, get up off your asses, pick up your shovel so we can make this the Promised Land."

6) Timothy 6:10—"For the love of money is the root of all evil."

7) Scripture—Idle hands are the Devil's workshop.

8) Lenin (1917) The State and Revolution—"He who does not work, neither shall he eat."

How does this all fit into Foreign policy? Well, Foreign Policy didn't come into existence until immediately after World War II to help rebuild Germany and Japan, and then just went wild trying to buy allies and friends worldwide to combat the "Evil Empire." Well, the Russians have straightened themselves out somewhat, so why are we spending Foreign Aid money? It certainly isn't getting to the people but, sure as hell, is lining the pockets of their leaders. Oh, now we are fighting terrorists. Well, go up to my list of 1-7 if we have sent Peace Corp people to show them how to grow food instead of sending money. They would be busy raising crops to feed their families instead of joining radical groups, which give them money to survive. This money is probably your tax dollars thereby cutting down on the number of terrorists. This writer thinks *it's a better spent dollar and a hell of a lot less dollars*. In another edition, I pointed out that 100 million acres of USA farmland was laying fallow due to drought and other crop failures. Why don't we draft the evicted farmers, into the Peace Corp and have them gone overseas to help teach other people how to farm. This gives us two bites at the apple so to speak: we take people who are probably on welfare and reduce that side of the ledger while paying them with foreign aid money which is taxable and add it to the income side of ledger.

We spent $53 million in foreign aid last year, which sure as "God made little green apples" never got to the people of those countries. Suppose we send grain instead under the supervision of the Peace Corp and not let the tribal chiefs or Honchos get their greedy little hands on it. We would be getting a bigger bang for our dollar and winning real friends whose rice bowl and bellies are full. Enough on Foreign Policy. Just talking or thinking about it makes me nauseated. We can change all of these ills in Washington, DC, by changing the way we send professional politicians and sending honest law abiding citizens which I outlined in previous editions.

Here is an old Italian story to close this part but very apropos : "Uncle Lucien and his Favorite Nephew Antonio." Whenever Antonio needed something, he would go see Uncle Lucien; and invariably, Uncle Lucien would say, "Sure, Antonio, get money in the drawer in the desk in the hall." After five or six times, Antonio again went to Uncle Lucien and got the same answer; but when he opened the drawer, the drawer was empty. Antonio said, "Uncle Lucien, there is nothing in the drawer." Uncle Lucien replied, "I know, Antonio. But if you had paid back every time you borrowed, it would be there."

This is a valuable lesson that everyone in the USA should learn—you cannot borrow forever!

PART 4

How about a bit on Amnesty?

To sum it up briefly, there are only three special interest groups who want Amnesty:

1) Politicians—to get votes.
2) Big Business—to get substandard wages.
3) Unions—to get additional membership as it's declining.

What do these three groups all have in common? Greed!

This author is fairly logical; however, this amnesty thing defies logic other than that cited above. Why would anyone in their right mind contemplate allowing somewhere between 11 million and 20 million illegal aliens gain legal status with so many Americans out of work? The big spread on the numbers is caused by whom you want to believe Department of Homeland Security which is naturally the lower or Boarder personnel and estimates by Bear Sterns which is the higher. I'll put my money on the Border personnel and Bear Sterns because anything that comes out of this administration isn't worth the powder to blow it away.

There was an interesting article in the *New York Times*. An illegal from Central America is working in New York as a laborer in a construction company for $25,000 a year under the table. Now the Comptroller's office for NYC says prevailing wage for this job is $39.25/hr or $81,640 per year. Geez, I wonder where the other $56,640 a year is going? There, my fellow Americans, is the problem with illegal aliens. It is difficult to get real numbers on this subject because it depends which side of the argument you are on, and what you are putting out to be the truth. I was finally able to get three sources to agree, two cited above, and "Citizens for law.org." These are very interesting numbers: for every one hundred illegal aliens sixty-five Americans are displaced from work. That being the case with 20 million illegals in this country divided by one hundred equals 200,000, and now times sixty-five Americans. Back to work would mean 13 million out of 22 million Americans would go back to work. That sure makes sense to this author, which means NO AMNESTY and deportation. Sorry, illegals, but you broke our immigration laws and do not deserve to be here, especially when you are hurting my fellow Americans. Adios, Amigo! Do not believe this hogwash about they are doing work that Americans won't do as that is nothing more than political rhetoric in favor of amnesty. Proof—The Center for Immigration Studies reports that in 2006 (which was George W. Bush administration) a sweeping raid of six Swift meat-packing plants in Minnesota, Nebraska, Texas, Colorado, and Utah about 1,300 illegal workers were arrested, and those jobs were filled by legal workers thereby disproving the rhetoric being fed to you; and remember jobs were plentiful at that time. It is way too long that politicians do things for re-election and not for the American people that they are supposedly serving. As this author feels just looking at the numbers above, putting 13million Americans back to work, should end all talk of amnesty in Washington, DC. A report from 2011 showed that illegals are costing this country 113 billion minimally plus 52 Billion for education of illegal children, etc., a year and growing. Now, one does not have to be a "rocket scientist " to see if we cut a minimum of 113 + 52 Billion annually and added income tax from 13 million working Americans, our deficit would start reversing very rapidly. Remember the illegals pay no income tax, and if they do, the Internal Revenue Service (IRS) refunds it plus a tax credit. It makes you feel really good that this country is so magnanimous and altruistic with our tax dollars and now wants more.

Saying this with tongue-in-cheek, this writer foresees an uprising in the making. Perhaps this is why Department of Homeland Security bought so much ammo because they see it also! In a recent speech, Senator Marco Rubio stated roughly, "We have to remember that illegals were real people with feelings and families," and I totally understand that. But guess what, Senator Rubio—"Americans are real people with feelings and families, and they belong here!" This is supposedly a nation of "Rule by Law"—so how can anyone justify granting amnesty to lawbreakers at the peril of real Americans?

Here's a little more information regarding illegal immigrants. Each year 72,000 illegals are arrested for drug offenses and represent 25 percent of the prison population. This is also costing you tax dollars because we don't deport them when caught but put them in our prisons. It's like they get a free ride for breaking the law. If that makes sense to anyone, please explain it to this author because it defies logic.

Just a little more info: approximately 400,000 illegals have been issued deportation orders and just disappeared at large in the United States of America with whereabouts unknown. Perhaps the illegals, when caught, should be given an implant so we can track them like we do livestock, right down to the stall number. Oh, I bet the American Civil Liberties Union will love that idea!

That's another subject but always understand that ACLU stood for American Civil Liberties Union. Then why are they screaming about profiling illegals and going to court to defend their rights, but they are not Americans. Get your heads on straight or change your name.

Fox Nation reports that the man currently sitting in the Oval Office and the Attorney General have broken seventeen immigration laws without permission from Congress. In addition, the Deputy Assistant Secretary of Department of Homeland Security stated in a call, "We're not doing raids or audits under this administration." Duh, what is happening, America: we are under MOB RULE!

Just to give you a comparison. In Mar 1945, we only had a little over 2,750,000 men in the army in European Theater Operations and we are looking at 20 million potential hostiles within our borders. If anyone doesn't see the potential for real problems on our soil, please run (don't walk) to the nearest eye doctor! Oh, it might be interesting to test how many states would be relieved of potential bankruptcy since the Feds pass on a huge amount of that cost directly back onto the state's budget and naturally their taxpayers.

"Truth is stranger than fiction, but it is because fiction is obliged to stick to possibilities. Truth isn't." (Mark Twain)

PART 5

Intermezzo—this writer believes that a book like this should have a section dedicated strictly to "stupid statements made by politicians only during its preparation" and general comments from the author:

1) Nancy Pelosi: "We didn't do this to Bush."

Well, Madam Pelosi, no, you didn't; however, Bush was a legal citizen of this country and was not attempting to shred our Constitution. On the other hand, Mr. Obama still hasn't demonstrated he is eligible to hold the office, and Mr. Obama continually breaks laws and tries to subvert the Congress plus is a disciple of Mr. Saul Alinsky—need I say more?

2) Nancy Pelosi: "The Republican approach does not prevent unacceptable and repeated abuses by Chairman Issa in any meaningful way."

Again Madam Pelosi, untimely death of anyone deserves to be looked at very carefully to be able to give closure to the families. They have a right to know whether or not they were just murdered by terrorist or their death were potentially avoidable due to inept government which they were serving and not the casual. What difference does it make now by your party's Secretary of State at the time, Mrs. Hillary Clinton!

3)   Senator Rockefeller of West Virginia. To suggest that over 200 million Americans are racists because of the president's color is inane and ridiculous. How about "it's a costly bad law?"

Being originally from New Jersey, we had a saying which belongs here "To call one is to be one" You don't deserve anymore of a response than that, sir.

4)   Mr. Obama: "Anything he says."

Sir, I, as an Independent, listened to your early primary speeches and early on determined "no way would you get my vote" primarily because of your Marxist lingo. After you were elected, much to my dismay, I stopped listening to anything you had to say. As a New Jersey breed boy, I knew "if your lips were moving, you were lying," which has proven to be true time and time again! Incidentally, you may be happy to know that my cooking and gardening skills have greatly improved as I immediately switch channels; so instead of listening to fictional rhetoric from you, I'm getting facts from knowledgeable people.

5)   Amusing little story: Neighbors, friends, and associates know I am an avid reader, and in particular, Nostradamus. Several times I've been queried as to whether or not Obama was the third Anti-Christ. To wit, I've responded emphatically: No! Nostradamus's Antichrist came out of Arabia not Kenya, and then they always bring up the "Blue Turban " bit he wore on July 26, 2008 in Berlin

and again, my response was that Mr. Obama is well read as are his handlers, and this writer's personal opinion was that it was nothing more than a political gimmick for he is only a showman at heart.

6) Terrorists are a worldwide problem; hence, my tendency would be to agree with Mr. Putin that these two countries should work together to eliminate the problem. Be aware that this is also presented in Nostradamus's quatrains as one interpretation.

PART 6

Deportation Incentives—this writer loves political clowns and who better than Nikita Khrushchev: "Call it what you will. Incentives are what get people to work harder." Using these words of true wisdom, I understand Canada is looking for workers to expand their production base:

1) Suppose we contacted our northern neighbor and got details on what they are looking for in the form of labor.

2) According to item twenty-seven in my first book "Open Letter to All Americans" on page 16, the Internal Revenue Service is ignoring Immigration and Naturalization Service / Immigration and Customs Enforcement Regulations relative to withholding information on illegal aliens. Well, let's put a stop to that immediately and share the information as required.

3) Now we offer illegals who have no felonies an incentive program:

   a) $1,000 to return to their country of origin, and they will get a clean shot at returning legally;

   b) If they qualify under Canada's criteria, we will pay for transportation to our northern border;

c) If they give us the name and address of another illegal, not in our computer system, an additional $250 per person and another $750 when they are captured;

d) If we have to come find you, you get nothing but a ride to the capital city of your origin via military cargo carrier;

e) If you are a felon in our prison system, you get a military cargo-plane ride to the capital city of your origin, and the party and freebies are over.

At best this plan can cost less than $10 billion, a considerable amount less than what we are paying out today.

The author feels this is a simple straightforward approach to solving the Illegal Alien problem and getting Americans back to work. Amnesty is nothing more than a political game for votes!

PART 7

Our Southern Border

Has anyone wondered why Obama is so lax on stiffening our southern border with Mexico? Or why he wants total amnesty? As mentioned previously, we have 20 million illegal aliens within our continental borders, which is a huge number; this coupled with the fact that Venezuela, with Russian financing has built an AK47 assault rifle factory and recently has up graded to the AK103 & AK104 rifles. Since Venezuela only has a standing army of approximately 110,000 men and are producing them at the rate of 25,000 a year. It can't be to equip its army; it would have been cheaper to buy the assault rifles. Hence, one must deduce that they will and/or are in the munitions business. Hmm, a socialistic country in a continent of predominantly socialistic governments. This writer, who was a trained intelligence analyst for Uncle Sam, smells trouble. The best part of being an analyst is you let your mind wander and assemble small bits and pieces of information to form a picture and/or an opinion of what's going to happen. In addition, reliable collateral information reports show 1,300,000 illegals crossed our southern border in very recent years from Central America and Mexico. I would hate to see another Pearl Harbor on US continental soil! Building a fence is almost as useless as teats on a boar hog. We need constant unpredictable drone flights over the entire length of this border. I remember seeing a picture of George W. Bush making an inspection, and the photographer caught in the picture two illegals successfully scaling the fence behind Bush's back. In addition to drone flights, we need infrared and regular camera surveillance for at least five miles below the border plus strategically placed subsurface sonic detectors. Drug cartels have already tunneled under the border successfully, so this is a must. I remember seeing a movie called *Red Dawn*, wherein the United States of America was successfully invaded through the southern border by hostiles armed in the movie with AK-47s. Much too much coincidental for this analyst! Remember there are people south of the border who charge illegals $150 just to show them when, where, and how to cross. Backing this up must be sufficient border guards and troops, if necessary, with the support of C-130 gunships a.k.a. Puff The Magic Dragon, etc., to assure no penetration. THEN AND ONLY THEN WILL BE ABLE TO FEEL COMFORTABLE IN OUR OWN HOMES.

PART 8

Too much government.

Using 2010 Federal census data, it has been relatively easy to determine that for every 69.5 American citizens, there is one federal employee; and for every 33.3 American citizens, there is one state employee—that's non-educational. Now you add to that County and Local where applicable all equals *too much government*. The people in Washington, DC, must recognize that the average taxpayer is being put between "the rock and a hard place." Now add to that expected political donations the charitable groups and churches: it leaves the taxpayer with very little disposable income. The size of Federal Government has been a debatable point since the Constitution was written and elaborated upon in Federalist Papers No. 37 and No. 45 very aptly mainly by James Madison and in No.19 Separation of Powers Federal and State by Thomas Jefferson when he very succinctly said, "I believe the States can best govern our home concerns and the General Government, our foreign ones." (Jefferson to William Johnson 1823.ME15:450) which about sums it all up. If the Federal Government makes a move, it's mirrored by the states i.e., Environmental Protection Agency-Department of Environmental Protection (EPA-DEP) and Florida Department of Transportation (FDOT)-State Department of Transportation (DOT): hence, there is collateral damage cost all the way back to the tax payer and always the taxpayer. Enough is Enough. As

Jefferson said, "Federal (a.k.a. General Government) foreign affairs." A lengthy mandate comes out of a federal agency and they are always lengthy. How do they know what conditions prevail in say New Jersey are not the same in Florida or Oregon. By stopping this absentee management style of government, we could potentially save a lot of duplication of efforts and there is duplication. Remember we are dealing with bureaucrats at all levels here all with the "PYOA mentality (protect your own ass)."

Back in 1982 the author had the privilege of serving on an Ad Hoc committee for then Governor Tom Kean of New Jersey (NJ) with specific instructions to develop a criteria for shortening the Development Process in New Jersey, which for a small subdivision, could take up to two years, provided you didn't have to deal with the state Department of Environmental Protection (DEP) which could add another eighteen months. We ended up doing this by increasing the watershed area approval by the county to keep it out of the Department of Environmental Protection and by passing legislation giving the state only Ninety days to approve and similar steps in the municipalities as New Jersey is a Home Rule State. That further developed unofficially into the $5, $10, and $25 reviews at county and state levels. You knew the character and quality of work to expect from each engineering firm; hence, the better more qualified firms drew a $5 review, so to speak, and the less qualified firms drew the $25 review. This unofficial system worked so well that my firm started introducing a fee structure into the municipality Land Improvement Code which went something like this: "The engineering review you receive on your initial submission will be all encompassing, and you are expected to complete every line item as specified. Should you not complete every line item, a second and/or third full review fee will be charged by the municipality." This system worked very well to the benefit of the municipality and to the detriment of the developer if he was using Mr. Joe Blow operating out of his house as a part time engineer. This writer feels probably this whole matter can be summed up as follows: If you feel like a hamburger, you put on your tee shirt and shorts and go to the Golden Arches. You don't put on a suit and tie and go to a restaurant with a maître d', a water boy, bread-and-butter boy, wine steward, and a waiter plus a bus boy and order a hamburger! This is what's happening in this country today with government, who because of absentee management, write everything long and lengthy to cover all possible situations. This current Administration has fewer businesspeople in its makeup than any other president; as a result, layer after layer of useless, idealistic regulations come out which do nothing more than hamper the economy, business, and industry. When does it all stop?

The enormous borrowing by the federal government doesn't help anyone or anybody except the people doing the loaning, and the drop in our financial rating can be contributed directly to this borrowing. The only thing growing in this country is food stamps and welfare because of this current administrations ridiculous policies, which must change.

This writer lives in a retirement community of over 1300 homes and to hear senior citizens rant and rave. I've stopped going to community functions, but it also exists in the local tavern or pub or restaurant, anywhere you go "the people are not happy." It causes me to take a pause and wonder: *where are we really going*? The only answer I can come up with is it's turning into a socialistic state by any other name you want to call it Liberalism or Obamaism. It must stop or I fear there will be a revolt like this country hasn't seen since the Revolutionary War, which was based on "Taxation without Representation, today." It will be "Taxation with Representation," the fallout of which this writer would hesitate to predict!

PART 9

Immigration Reform

(Data derived from closeup.org/immigration.htm July1998)

Today, the United States of America has the most liberal Immigration Policy in the entire world:

1) started in 1790 and being wide open to stopping immigration from China in 1862;
2) to baring all Asians in 1870;
3) to restricting to 3 percent residents from that country currently living in the United States in 1921;
4) to Deportation of Mexicans in 1924 due to depression;
5) to exclusion of all foreigners in 1941;
6) to refugees from Europe in1948;
7) to barring possible communists in 1952;
8) to allowing Cuban refugees in 1959;
9) to Vietnamese refugees for possible persecution in 1980, etc.

This is basically a living document dealing with specific times and conditions.

The current 1998 Policy is broken down into basically 4 sections:

1) Family-Sponsored Immigrants: up to 480,000 in four specific categories
2) Employment-Based Immigrants: up to 140,000 visas in five preference categories
3) Diversity Immigrants: up to 55,000 visas primarily from countries that are not currently principal sources in six geographical regions.
4) Refugees and Asylees: persons outside of their country who can't or will not return to country of origin. This is an arbitrary number determined by the President in consultation with Congress with the 1998 authorization being set at 83,000.

When in business, the only sections this writer encountered problems with were Category 2 sections dealing with immigrants with "advanced degrees and skilled workers, other professionals, and other workers" since the Federal government from time to times strikes deals with particular countries to allow 20,000 to 30,000 in those two sections cited above into this country. In the early 1970s, things were slow workwise, and yet Immigration Naturalization Service (INS) / Immigration and Customs Enforcement (ICE) was encouraging consultants to hire people in these particular sections over Americans, which from a business stand point made perfect sense when you could hire someone with the licensing required at half the price. Then about ten years later, similar set of work conditions had an employee from Jamaica on a work visa which had run out, unbeknown to me, and in our particular field due to the high fluctuation of work many responsible, Americans had fled the workforce field. They actually had to sponsor the Jamaican to get him back on payroll but not until having to go through a ton and a half of INS paperwork. Nonetheless, it seems to point out a significant point relative to our immigration policies that they should be tied to our unemployment number in an inverse percentage to the immigration maximums. *Businessweek* states that a full employment number for the USA is between 3 percent and 4 percent of total workforce; hence, at that point of 3 to 4 percent full employment should equal 100 percent on immigration numbers. This writer's opinion would be that this would be the fairest to all concerned and verified monthly.

PART 10

Comments

You, the reader, must be wondering why a seventy-five-year-old man, who is both a father and grandfather, would take the time to write three short books on the ills of this great Nation. For just the reason stated above, I grew up in the land of the free; I have been a law-abiding citizen, served my country and my communities, and want my three children and six grandchildren and yours to also grow up and live their lives free as God intended man to be. I was instilled with patriotism by our Founding Fathers' great sacrifice, brilliance, and courage to create a free Nation and to see it being torn asunder by politics and all of its fallacies, tears my heart and soul.

We all red-blooded, real Americans, regardless of race, creed, or color, helped build this nation, no matter how large or small our individual contribution may have been; it was a toiling effort and to see it being put into a tailspin by greedy merchants—is beyond my ability to control my temper any longer.

The only answer lies in the Constitution by which we are governed, not by what we are being told by politicians or not told by the mass media nor by people who feel the Constitution, which is our basis for freedom, is old fashion and needs to be rewritten. NOT on my life will that occur nor should it be on your life, we must start a grassroots movement that will shake Washington, DC, to its core. No, I'm not a Tea Party member; but they have the right idea, which is a grassroots movement to stop all the nonsense -and-business-as- usual in our Capital. No, they are not a political party but Independents and hold fifty-one seats in the House of Representatives.

We have got to get that number up higher and in this election, in 2014, we must take control of the Senate as the 113th congress has been hampered by the Democratic control in the Senate.

I am personally appalled at Obama's recent announcement that he wants to change the 22nd amendment so that he can seek a third term in 2016. It is my opinion that should that happen we will all be calling one another comrade and spending tax dollars to build a mosque in every major city, or be all working for the Federal Government or both. He has the audacity to suggest that he's at par with Franklin D. Roosevelt (FDR). Well, that shows what conceit will do. He lies continually on any subject at any time to further his Left Wing agenda that will break the United States of America as we know it. His big money are the Unions and George Soros, a scoundrel of the first order, so much so that Russia has issued an International warrant for his arrest as a financial terrorist and convicted felon and Obama says, "Can't be the same guy." Believe me it is! In previous writings, I let you people know what type of individual Mr. Soros is and was—not a pretty or respectable story. What's that old saying "Birds of the same feather flock together"? Obama and Soros.

I'm not a lawyer but based on all the evidence witnessed by this writer, Mr. Obama is an impostor and under the Constitution is ineligible to serve as president as both parents were not American Citizens and born on United States soil. I am totally confused by Supreme Court of the United States and its apparent unwillingness to hear case after case regarding this subject initially believing it was because of his color that they were reluctant to hear, but then they made critical decisions in segregation cases and granted different members are currently serving. Then there was the possibility they were concerned about social upheaval, but they're not supposed to enter into it. So am I at a loss as to why!

Mr. Obama is a disciple of Mr. Saul Alinsky who wrote "Rules for Radicals" back in the 60s: that volatile period in American history with anti-war demonstrations and the civil rights movement; and along came Alinsky who was such a rabble rouser that the police used to arrest him and put him in jail when he showed up in any city or town. Very coincidentally, this portion of this PART 10 is being written on Memorial Day after having concluded a moment of silent prayer for the one million Americans who paid the supreme price—their lives, so that we can enjoy the freedoms we hold so dear.

This writer is not prone to "crying wolf." However, the time is here to say "BEWARE, AMERICA—Cerberus (Greek mythical three-headed dog that guards the gates of hell) is roaming free in this Continental United States of America using the name Barack Hussein Obama." Yes indeed. One head claims to be President of the United States of America, an office which he illegally holds; the second head pretends to be an American when he is really an Alinsky Marxist; and the third head claims to be a Christian when, in reality, he is Muslim to the core, and the snakes on his mane spew nothing but Socialism a.k.a. Liberalism.

Proof:

1) In 2010 he forced the "Affordable Health Care Act" through Congress which happens to be Rule 1 in Alinsky's "Rules for Radicals";

2) He constantly violates our Constitution and apparently holds it with such disdain that he pushes for rule by International Law a.k.a. One World Government;

3) He pushes for gun control—a direct violation of our Second Amendment;

4) He tries to control mass media—a direct violation of our First Amendment. Fortunately, some mass media just aren't buying into it;

5) He is purging our Military of its top leadership—reminiscent of the Soviet Union's Great Purge of 1934-1940. Since 2011, sixteen top-commanding generals, two admirals, fifty-six naval officers and in 2013, twenty naval officers plus 157 air force majors (Conservative Angle). The Russian purge almost cost them their entire country to the Germans because of top military leadership;

6) Since his election in 2008, 8 million jobs have been lost to American workers;

7) Food stamp and welfare roles have swelled under his Alinsky-styled policies;

8) His low moral standard relative to homosexuality and lying—this writer is amazed he hasn't said the Ten Commandments were also outdated as he has said our Constitution is;

9) We, Americans, must meet this threat head on and return this serial bully who struts around this country, not caring one iota about its people from whence it came.

Abraham Lincoln once said, "I am a firm believer in the people. If given the truth, they can be depended upon to meet any national crisis. The great point is to bring them the real facts."

You herein have been presented with the true facts, so together we can begin "a journey of a thousand miles began with a single step (1904 Lao Tzu)." That first step is the 2014 Congressional elections and your vote for Independents or Republicans. We must turn out every Democratic candidate (a.k.a. Obama Cronies) so we can restore this Nation back to its natural God-given glory, return our American workers back to work, and end this insanity currently going on in our Nation's Capital. All the items recommended by this writer can be accomplished by us all taking this first big step in November!

God Bless, and may we—the people—be victorious at the polls!

INDEX